Beethoven's 5th Symphony

Arranged by Wesley Schaum

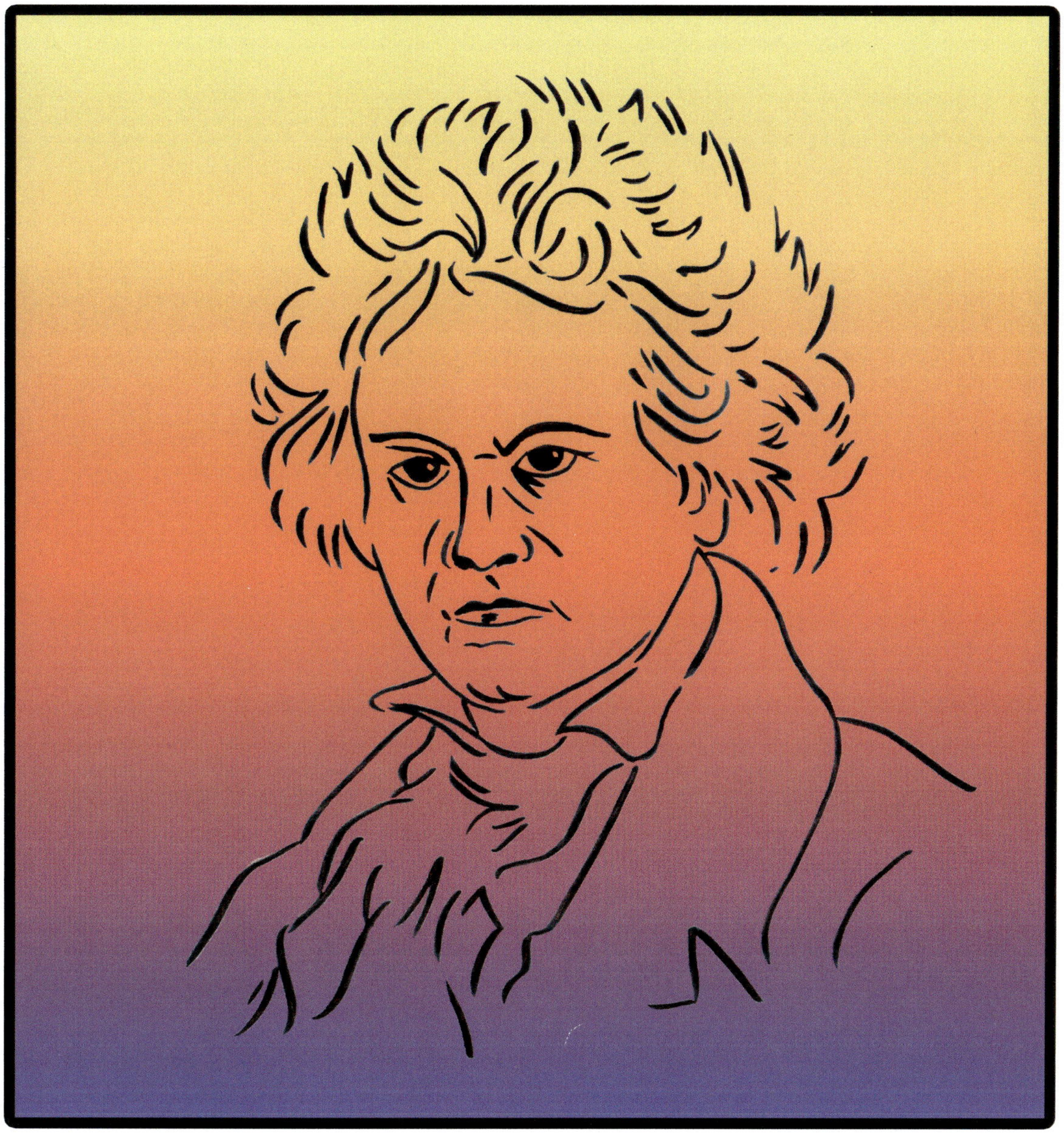

Beethoven's 5th Symphony

First Movement

Andante ♩ = 80-84

Ludwig van Beethoven, Op. 67
arr. by Wesley Schaum

Schaum Publications, Inc. • 10235 N. Port Washington Rd. • Mequon, WI 53092 • www.schaumpiano.net

25
1
2
p
4
1
3
1
2
30
2
2
2
2
2
1
2
1
3
1
35
5
3
ff
f
2
4
1
40
5
mf
2
1
4
3
1
4
45
4
2
f
ff
1
8vb

EXCLUSIVELY DISTRIBUTED BY

HAL•LEONARD® CORPORATION

7777 W. BLUEMOUND RD. P.O. BOX 13819 MILWAUKEE, WI 53213

U.S. $3.99

0 08148 05871 6

HL00645626

Level Three